A YEAR ON THE ROAD TO NOWHERE

WRITTEN BY

Jessie Hale

ILLUSTRATED BY

John Soleas

January

In January, the sun is only out for a few hours a day in Iqaluit.

I'm usually the only one walking on the Road to Nowhere, but I see lots of snowmobiles on the land.

February

February is the coldest month of the year.

I have to wear my long underwear, leggings, warm socks, snow pants, sweater, and parka. Then I put on my goggles, face mask, hat, and mitts. Phew!

March

March is a beautiful month. There is lots of sunlight and lots of snow. I think the land looks so bright and clean.

April

In April, the Road to Nowhere opens up to trucks and cars. I start to see people driving out to the gun range.

May

In May, the birds come back. I see ducks, Canada geese, and lots of snow buntings!

June

There is still snow in June, but it's light out almost all the time. I can go for a walk any time of day!

July

In July, it seems like everyone in town has a tent up.

In the evenings, I can see bonfires everywhere I look.

August

In August, beautiful flowers line the Road to Nowhere. Purple and yellow are my favourite colours.

September

September is the time for berry picking! The more snow there is in the winter, the more berries there will be in the fall.

October

In October, the days get shorter and there is more snow. I watch as the last tents come down.

November

We get the first blizzards in November. It is not fun to walk outside when it's windy!

December

In December, it is dark out most of the time. I can only go for walks in the middle of the day.